Appetizers

Hilary,
Enjoy !! :)
Love.
Chelsea
2009 ~

Published originally in Italian as *Antipasti*
© 2005 **Food Editore srl**
Via Vittor Pisani, 5 - 20124 MILAN, ITALY
Via Mazzini, 6 - 43100 PARMA, ITALY

English Translation
Traduzioni Culinarie

Photographs
Alberto Rossi and Davide Di Prato

Recipes
Simone Rugiati and Licia Cagnoni

Thanks to
I Love My House (Barazzoni, Parma)

This 2008 edition printed exclusively for Barnes & Noble, Inc.,
by Food Editore srl.

ISBN-13: 978-1-4351-0620-8

Printed and bound in China
10 9 8 7 6 5 4 3 2 1

Appetizers

Great Recipes from the Chefs of Food Editore

Parma, Milan

Contents

Basic Techniques

THE TRADITION OF APPETIZERS

The Italian word *antipasto* means "before the meal," and these appetizers can be some of the most interesting dishes to make and enjoy. They can be served with drinks, as main courses, or as side dishes—they can even constitute a whole meal.

Small and quick to make, hors d'oeuvres are particularly suited to buffet lunches and cocktail parties, where guests help themselves directly from platters. These little snacks can be called finger food, tapas, or *mise en bouche*, but whatever the name, the concept remains the same: individual nibbles such as mini pizzas, small quiches, or little croquettes requiring no cutlery.

This book presents a wide selection of appetizers, made with meat, fish, and vegetables, served warm, cold, cooked, and raw. One word of advice: Appetizers should be the lightest dish of the meal, so it's best to start with more delicate flavors and finish with stronger, heartier foods, creating a crescendo of tastes and textures.

Appetizers boast a long tradition in the history of gastronomy, with even the ancient Romans beginning their meals with light dishes, called *gustio* or *gustatio* (hard-boiled eggs were traditional), served with a wine and honey drink called *mulsum*.

Throughout the ages appetizers have appeared in different positions in the sequence of dishes. However, today as a general rule they are served before the soup. In the Italian gastronomic tradition, the number of appetizers has been greatly reduced, and now there are usually no more than two different dishes.

Italian antipasti par excellence include *salumi* (different kinds of cured meat, often pork), two classics being prosciutto di Parma and *culatello di Zibello*. When salumi are fresh and somewhat mild, they are best with salted bread; if they are aged, spicy, or possessing a pronounced flavor, they should be served with a blander pairing, such as unsalted Tuscan bread. If you can, try to slice salumi by hand or with a manual slicing machine. Because of its high speed, an electric slicing machine tends to heat up and melt the salumi fat, which should melt only in the mouth.

Antipasti made with fish are also very popular; these can include traditional smoked salmon, served on buttered toasts; anchovies in salt, oil, or a marinade; and seafood salad.

Regional Italian cuisines offer many specialties, such as chickpea *panelle* and croquettes from Palermo seasoned with lemon, the Piedmontese anchovy and garlic dip *bagna caoda*, stuffed fried olives from Ascoli Piceno, Tuscan chicken liver crostini, and Sicilian *arancini* (rice balls).

There are some countries where appetizers, or small dishes, are as important as any other course, if not more so. For example in Scandinavia, particularly in Sweden, *smorgasbord*, "board of bread," is a complete meal.

One starts with different kinds of fish and shellfish, moving on to cured and smoked meats, then finishing with warm foods. The whole meal is served with different types of bread, including typical rye crispbread, as well as salads and very strong alcohol.

In Russia *zakuski* includes piroshki (filled puffs or pastries), caviar and other fish roes, small pieces of rye bread with sauerkraut and smoked goose, potato and beet salads, and different kinds of smoked or marinated fish.

Another well-known selection of small dishes are mezes, native to Lebanon but now widespread throughout the Middle East. These reflect not only a gastronomic tradition, but a whole way of looking at life. They consist of a series of little dishes (anywhere from four to forty), all served with a dry spirit made of anise, called *arak*, which is diluted with water and ice. Hummus (chickpea dip), falafel (chickpea fritters), dolmades (grape leaves stuffed with rice), fried pastries filled with meat or cheese, *taramosalata* (creamy fish roe spread), and a yogurt, cucumber, and garlic sauce called *tzatziki* in Greece are just some of the most popular meze dishes. Mezes represent an important opportunity for people to gather together—sometimes for many hours.

BASIC DOUGHS

Puff Pastry

This pastry makes an ideal base for many recipes. It's light and flaky and can be used to prepare many different dishes, both savory and sweet.

Ingredients

1²⁄₃ cups (7 ounces) all-purpose flour

7 tablespoons water

1 pinch salt

1 cup (9 ounces) butter, cut into small pieces

Method

Mound the flour on a work surface, make a well in the center, then add the water and salt. Mix together until smooth, then wrap in a clean kitchen towel and let rest for 20 minutes.

Roll out the dough with a rolling pin to a square ¼-inch thick. Place the butter in the middle, fold over the dough, and close it completely, forming a parcel. Roll out gently with the rolling pin, then wrap the dough in foil and refrigerate for 5 minutes.

Unwrap the dough and place on the work surface. Roll it out into a long strip (about ½-inch thick). Fold a third in toward the middle, then cover it with another third, to form three layers of dough. Turn it around 90 degrees, then roll the dough out again into a long strip. Fold it again in thirds, then wrap in foil and refrigerate for about 30 minutes. Repeat two more times.

When completed, leave the dough to rest in the refrigerator for at least an hour before using.

Chef's Secrets

To make good puff pastry, it is important to have all the ingredients at the same temperature, so they blend together well.

The butter in particular should be at the same temperature as the dough. If it's too cold, it could make the dough crumble, while if it is too warm it could be too runny.

Before baking, score the top of the dough, making a small hole so that steam can escape without dampening the pastry too much.

To brown the dough, brush it with lightly beaten egg or milk before placing in the oven.

Cooking Tips

Puff pastry is one of the most versatile doughs, as it can be used in both savory and sweet recipes. With respect to hors d'oeuvres, it is very useful for shaping rolls or small baskets for mousses and savory sauces and to prepare vol-au-vents, small pastry parcels filled with vegetables and béchamel, or savory pies and tarts.

Puff pastry is also well suited for topping baked vegetable pies. Last but not least, it can be rolled out thinly and covered with herbs or spices to make crispy, flaky crackers.

Pâte Brisée

Ingredients

2½ cups (10½ ounces)
   all-purpose flour
¼ cup (½ stick) butter
1 pinch salt
1 egg
1 tablespoon extra-virgin olive oil
7 tablespoons lukewarm water

Method

Mound flour, butter, and salt on a work surface. Make a well in the middle, then add the egg, olive oil, and lukewarm water.

Mix and knead the ingredients until they form a soft and elastic dough. Wrap in plastic wrap and refrigerate.

Cooking Tips

Pâte brisée is savory short pastry, mainly used as a base for pies, tarts, small rolls, and many other different forms that are filled and baked after being brushed with beaten egg or milk.

The pâte brisée can be given extra flavor and crispness by being sprinkled with sesame, poppy, or any other kind of seed before baking.

Chef's secrets

It's very important to have the butter and eggs at room temperature and to work the dough quickly so as not to overheat the butter, which could compromise the dough's elasticity. Let the dough rest in the refrigerator for at least 30 minutes, to allow the ingredients to blend together well.

If you use pâte brisée as a base for savory pies, be sure to prick the base with a fork to prevent it from puffing up during baking and ruining the pie. Pâte brisée can be kept in the refrigerator for a couple of days, wrapped in foil. Alternatively, it can be frozen and then slowly thawed out before using.

Cannoncini

This is a recipe for simple yet delicious savory cannoncini, little rolls that can be stuffed with any number of ingredients. These pastry rolls are convenient, as they can be prepared in advance and filled later. For frying, they must be rolled around cylindrical stainless steel molds.

Method

Roll the pâte brisée out on a work surface. Use a cutting wheel or sharp knife to cut it into strips the width of the cylindrical molds, with an extra ¾ inch for closing the rolls.

Brush the edge of the strip with a little beaten egg white, then wrap the dough around the mold and press the edges together to seal.

Heat an abundance of sunflower oil (or other vegetable oil), then fry the pastry rolls (see below). Drain and dry well on paper towels.

Cooking Tips

The fried and cooled cannoncini can be filled with ricotta cheese mixed with oil, oregano, salt and pepper, with a spoonful of diced tomato and fresh basil in the middle; or try fillings prepared with white fish, such as grouper or cod, flavored with aromatic herbs and lemon zest.

Chef's Secrets

Remove the pastry dough from any wrapping and knead it gently before the surface becomes dry and crumbly, or wrap it in a slightly damp kitchen towel to stop it from drying out. Phyllo dough can also be used for baked snacks or crackers. It should be rolled out very thinly and served with fresh cheese and vegetable mousses.

SAUCES

Sauces and mousses can be used as fillings for canapés, toppings for bruschetta (toast seasoned with olive oil and garlic), the stuffing of savory puffs, or as dips for raw and steamed vegetables. These basic sauces are precious allies, helping enhance the flavors of many culinary creations.

Ricotta Cream with Ginger and Chives
Ingredients
1 cup (7 ounces) fresh ricotta

1 tablespoon extra-virgin olive oil

salt and pepper

1 tablespoon grated ginger

chives, minced

Method
Pass the fresh ricotta through a sieve, then beat it with a spatula until it becomes a soft, smooth cream with no lumps; stir in the extra-virgin olive oil and salt and pepper to taste. Gently squeeze the ginger between your fingers so that the juice drips into the ricotta. Stir in the chives and refrigerate for an hour before serving.

Yogurt Dip
Ingredients
2 tablespoons minced fresh herbs
  (parsley, dill, oregano, basil)

1 ¾ cups Greek yogurt

2 garlic cloves, minced

2 tablespoons honey

1 teaspoon salt

black pepper

½ teaspoon paprika

salt

Method
Mix the salmon and onion with the cheese; season with paprika and salt. Refrigerate for 1 hour, then use to fill tarts or vol-au-vents.

Ham Mousse
Ingredients
2 cups chopped ham

¼ cup (½ stick) butter plus extra
  for coating mold

4 ½ teaspoons all-purpose flour

½ cup milk

salt and pepper

nutmeg

¾ cup heavy cream

Method
Mix all of the ingredients in a bowl until smooth. Pass through a sieve, then refrigerate overnight. This dip can be served with seasonal vegetables or used as a sauce or salad dressing.

Smoked Salmon Cream
Ingredients
3 ounces smoked salmon

1 white onion, minced

7 ounces robiola cheese or other fresh,
  creamy cheese

Method

Puree the ham in a food processor. Melt 1 tablespoon of the butter in a saucepan. Remove from heat and add the flour. Return the saucepan to the heat and cook briefly, stirring constantly. Gradually pour in the milk and simmer, then add salt, pepper, and a grating of nutmeg.

Remove the béchamel from the heat and stir in the ham. Pass the mixture through a sieve.

Whip the cream until stiff, beat the remaining butter until soft, then combine the cream and butter with the ham mixture.

Pour into a buttered mold and refrigerate for 3 to 4 hours.

This delicate mousse can be spread on crackers or bread.

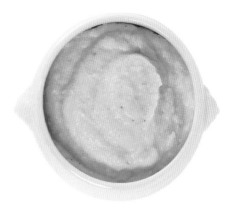

Mustard Mayonnaise

Ingredients

1 egg yolk
1 tablespoon mild mustard
1 tablespoon balsamic vinegar
½ cup sunflower oil
1 tablespoon extra-virgin olive oil
salt and pepper

Method

Beat the egg yolk and mustard in a bowl, then gradually add the balsamic vinegar. Mix together the oils, then gradually add them to the egg yolk, first drop by drop, and then in a very thin stream, whisking constantly. Season to taste with salt and pepper.

This mayonnaise can serve as a flavorful dip for raw vegetables and makes a great alternative to butter when preparing smoked fish canapés.

Hollandaise

Ingredients

¾ cup vinegar
salt and pepper
1 tablespoon vegetable stock
2 egg yolks
½ cup (1 stick) butter, cut into pieces
1 tablespoon all-purpose flour

Method

Place the vinegar in a small saucepan with salt and pepper and bring to a boil. Reduce to about half the original volume, then remove from the heat and cool until tepid.

Stir in the stock, egg yolks, and half the butter. Place the saucepan over another saucepan of boiling water (bain-marie) and whisk the ingredients together. Add the remaining butter, the flour, and a little cold water, whisking constantly. Pass the sauce through a sieve to remove any lumps. Keep it warm over a bain-marie until ready to serve.

APPETIZER PRESENTATION

As the first dish to be served, appetizers need to whet the appetite for what comes next. Their appeal should be to both the palate and the eye. Colors should be vivid, aromas should seduce, and flavors should awaken the imagination. Great attention should be paid to presentation—almost as much as to preparation in the kitchen.

Etiquette books suggest serving appetizers on small plates that can be easily filled, while giving the impression of being generous. Canapés and crostini should be served on separate trays so guests can help themselves with their fingers. Olives should be served in a small bowl together with a spoon, while sardines and caviar should be on a plate with a little scoop. Pâtés should be presented on a plate with a flat knife.

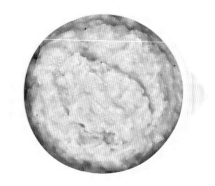

Molded appetizers look more attractive if served in individual portions on a bed of salad or herbs, together with an aromatic, colorful sauce.

Creams and pâtés can be spread on little slices of bread or toast and become even more appealing when piped using a pastry bag, or arranged in cups or bowls made from carved fruits or vegetables.

Cured meats are particularly suited to being rolled on breadsticks or vegetable spears, or stuffed with various fillings.

Hors d'oeuvres are very convenient because most can be prepared in advance. Terrines and pâtés should be prepared a day in advance to let the flavors develop; this approach applies to most creams and sauces, as well. However, all should be removed from the refrigerator at least 30 minutes before serving. Savory pies, quiches, and tarts can be reheated a few minutes before serving.

We hope this brief introduction has shown you how dishes of the highest quality can be served with a minimum of stress.

Meat, Cheese, and Vegetables

In the following pages, you'll find
original ideas for appetizers featuring
cured meats and cheeses, as well as
lighter vegetable-based options.

Roasted Vegetables in Puff Pastry

Serves 4

½ cup extra-virgin olive oil
1 garlic clove
½ white onion, chopped
1 cup (7 ounces) diced pumpkin
½ yellow bell pepper, diced
½ red bell pepper, diced
salt and pepper
8 small zucchini, diced
8 cherry tomatoes, diced
oregano
1 roll of puff pastry (5½ ounces)

Preparation time 20 minutes
Cooking time 30 minutes
Level easy
Wine Charmat method, fresh and light-bodied sparkling wine,
such as Prosecco di Conegliano Brut

Preheat oven to 400°F.

Heat the oil in a frying pan with the unpeeled garlic clove. Add the onion and sauté for 3 minutes. Add the pumpkin, then the peppers. Season lightly with salt, then cook for 6 to 7 minutes, adding a little water if necessary. Add the zucchini and tomatoes, sprinkle with oregano and a little pepper, and continue cooking until all of the vegetables are tender, about ten minutes.

Meanwhile cut the puff pastry into four circles of 2½ inches in diameter. Lay them over four upside-down semispherical molds (or ovenproof teacups). Bake for 10 minutes. Remove from the oven, take the pastry off the molds, and use the pastry as baskets in which to serve the hot vegetables.

Polenta Trio

Serves 4

1 carrot, peeled and diced
1 zucchini, green part only, diced
1 stalk of celery, diced
6 tablespoons extra-virgin olive oil
1 cup (9 ounces) instant polenta
2 tablespoons black olives in oil
3 tablespoons diced tomatoes
oregano
1 fresh porcini mushroom
1 garlic clove, smashed
fresh thyme
salt and pepper

Preparation time 35 minutes
Cooking time 25 minutes
Level easy
Wine young, light-bodied red without too much structure,
such as Friuli Merlot

Sauté the carrot, zucchini, and celery in a drizzle of olive oil for 2 minutes.

Bring a small saucepan of salted water to a boil and add 2 tablespoons of olive oil. Gradually whisk in the polenta and cook for a few minutes. Pour ¾ of the polenta into a plastic rectangular mold or container to make a ¼-inch thick layer. Stir the sautéed vegetables into the remaining polenta.

In a small frying pan sauté the olives with a little olive oil, the tomatoes, and oregano. Clean the mushroom well, then dice and sauté in a frying pan with a little olive oil, the garlic, thyme, and salt and pepper. Once the sheet of polenta has cooled, cut into circles and triangles using cookie cutters.

Heat some olive oil in a frying pan and fry the polenta triangles.

Sear the polenta circles in a nonstick frying pan.

Use an ice-cream scoop or melon baller to make four balls of the polenta and vegetable mixture.

Compose individual plates, each with a ball of polenta and vegetables, a polenta triangle topped with the olives and tomatoes, and a polenta circle topped with sautéed mushroom.

Vegetable Sushi

Serves 4

1 cup (5 ounces) white sushi rice
2-inch piece kombu seaweed
1 teaspoon sugar
2 tablespoons rice wine vinegar
4 sheets nori seaweed
2 tablespoons tahini
1 carrot, julienned
1 zucchini, julienned
1 radicchio heart, shredded

Preparation time 20 minutes
Cooking time 12 minutes
Level easy
Wine Champagne with good body and structure and intense bouquet, such as Champagne Brut Côte de Bar

Boil the rice in water with the piece of kombu for 12 minutes.

Dissolve the sugar in the rice wine vinegar. Remove the kombu, and let the rice sit and absorb water. Then stir in the rice wine vinegar mixture, and let sit for 10 minutes.

Toast the nori seaweed directly over (not on) a stovetop burner.

With dampened hands, spread the rice over the sheets of seaweed. Brush with tahini, then arrange the vegetables in the middle of the rice. Roll up the sushi using a bamboo mat. Dampen the edge of the seaweed with a little cold water and press to seal.

Refrigerate for 30 minutes, then cut into slices and serve.

Spring Onions with Egg Sauce

Serves 4

Spring onions
24 tender spring onions, peeled and trimmed
½ cup (1 stick) butter
½ cup (3 ½ ounces) grated Parmesan cheese

Egg sauce
4 eggs
salt
½ cup chicken broth
Parmesan cheese, grated

Garnish
½ duja salami or other soft salami, crumbled
extra-virgin olive oil

Preparation time 15 minutes
Cooking time 10 minutes
Level easy
Wine young, medium-bodied white with evolved bouquet of yellow fruits,
such as Alto Adige Sauvignon Blanc

Cook the spring onions in salted boiling water until tender, then drain.

Melt the butter in an ovenproof frying pan and sauté the spring onions. Cover with the Parmesan and place under the broiler or grill until browned.

In a heavy frying pan, fry the eggs. Sprinkle with salt and puree in a food processor with the broth and a handful of grated Parmesan.

In another frying pan, sauté the salami with a drizzle of oil until browned.

Arrange the spring onions on a plate and garnish with the egg sauce and the salami.

Cook's tip Duja is a Piedmontese salami made from pork, weighing about 7 ounces. Its name comes from the way it is preserved: the salami is immersed in a terracotta vessel (known as a *duja*) full of melted lard. Once it has hardened, the lard keeps the salami soft for several months. This preservation method also helps the salami develop its characteristic spicy flavor.

Leek and Truffle Panzerotti

Serves 4

Dough
1 cup (4½ ounces) all-purpose flour
3 tablespoons extra-virgin olive oil
1 pinch salt
3 tablespoons, plus 1½ teaspoons water
1 teaspoon lard

Filling
2 tablespoons butter
1 small leek, thinly sliced
3½ ounces whole-wheat bread
¾ cup milk
1 tablespoon truffle oil
1 white truffle, thinly sliced
salt and pepper
sunflower oil for frying

Preparation time 25 minutes
Cooking time 15 minutes
Level easy
Wine young, medium-bodied rosé with floral, fruity aromas,
such as Veneto Bardolino Chiaretto

Pour the flour into a bowl and add the olive oil, salt, water, and lard. Mix the ingredients together thoroughly, then transfer to a work surface and knead until the dough is smooth and elastic. Wrap in plastic wrap and refrigerate.

Heat the butter in a frying pan and sauté the leek, adding a little water if necessary, until translucent.

Soak the bread in the milk until soft, then drain and squeeze out excess liquid.

Mix together the soaked bread, sautéed leek, and truffle oil. Add half the truffle and season to taste with salt and pepper.

Roll out the dough and cut into circles. Stuff the circles with the leek mixture and seal the edges.

Heat the sunflower oil until very hot, then fry the stuffed dough until golden. Serve the panzerotti with the remaining truffle slices.

Zucchini and Pecorino Tarts

Serves 4

1 tablespoon extra-virgin olive oil
1 garlic clove, smashed
3 zucchini, cut into matchsticks
salt and pepper
4 tablespoons corn oil
2 tablespoons slivered almonds
5 ounces mild pecorino, shaved
9 ounces puff pastry (see page 8)

Preparation time 20 minutes
Cooking time 25 minutes
Level easy
Wine young, light-bodied white with grassy, fresh-fruit bouquet,
such as Piedmont Roero Arneis

Preheat oven to 375°F.

Heat the olive oil in a frying pan and sauté the garlic until brown. Remove and discard, then add the zucchini and sauté over high heat for 5 minutes. Season to taste with salt and pepper.

Brush small individual tart tins with corn oil, then spread a layer of almonds in each. Add the zucchini and a few pecorino shavings to each tin.

Cut the puff pastry into 4 circles the same diameter as the tins. Lay the circles over the zucchini and press down gently. Bake for 15 minutes.

Remove from the oven and take the tarts out of the tins by turning each upside down.

Pork, Savoy Cabbage, and Carrot Terrine

Serves 4

Terrine
2 tablespoons raisins
¼ cup Marsala wine
4 Savoy cabbage leaves, from the heart of the cabbage
3 carrots, peeled
1½ cups (14 ounces) ground pork
½ cup (4 ounces) diced soft salami
3 tablespoons extra-virgin olive oil
salt and black pepper

Garnish
7 tablespoons balsamic vinegar

Preparation time 20 minutes
Cooking time 50 minutes
Level medium
Wine medium-structured red with evolving bouquet of ripe red fruits,
such as Piedmont Nebbiolo d'Alba

Preheat oven to 375°F.
 Soak the raisins in the Marsala.
 Blanch the cabbage leaves in salted boiling water, then drain and let cool on a clean kitchen towel.
 Steam or boil the carrots until tender, then julienne.
 Mix the minced pork with the salami, extra-virgin olive oil, salt, pepper, and drained raisins.
 Line a terrine mold with waxed paper and fill it with alternating layers of meat, cabbage, and carrots. Press down well and place in a bain-marie (water bath) and bake for 20 minutes.
 Meanwhile reduce the balsamic vinegar over low heat until thickened.
 Remove the terrine from the oven, let sit for a few minutes, then serve, sliced, drizzled with the reduced vinegar.

Poached Pork over White Bean Puree

Serves 4

Pork
2 celery stalks, chopped
1 carrot, chopped
1 red onion, chopped
2 bay leaves
4 sage leaves
1 rosemary sprig
5 juniper berries
coarse salt
2 cups medium-bodied white wine
14 ounces pork shoulder or neck

White bean puree
1 cup (7 ounces) cannellini beans, soaked overnight
coarse salt
3 garlic cloves
2 tablespoons extra-virgin olive oil
sage
salt and black pepper

Garnish
sunflower oil for frying
1 yellow onion, thinly sliced into rings

Preparation time 25 minutes
Cooking time 1 hour
Level easy
Wine young, sparkling red with intense fragrance of violets,
such as Emilia-Romagna Lambrusco

Place the celery, carrot, red onion, bay leaves, sage, rosemary, and juniper berries in a saucepan. Cover with 4 cups (1 quart) water, add salt, and bring to a boil. Add the wine and then the whole piece of meat. Simmer for about 30 minutes, then remove from the heat and let the pork cool in its cooking liquid.

Cook the cannellini beans in salted boiling water with the whole, unpeeled garlic cloves until beans are tender. Remove and discard the garlic, drain the beans, and puree them in a food processor with the olive oil, sage, salt, and pepper until smooth.

Heat the sunflower oil until hot, then fry the onion rings until golden and crispy.

Drain the pork and shred by hand into small pieces. Serve the pieces on top of dollops of bean puree and garnish with the fried onions.

Spicy Lentil Pâté

Serves 4

1 cup (7 ounces) dried lentils
6 tablespoons extra-virgin olive oil
1 garlic clove
1 cup (4 ounces) minced celery, carrot, and onion
1 teaspoon curry powder
1 teaspoon tomato paste
2 cups hot vegetable broth
salt and pepper
1 tablespoon minced parsley

Preparation time 30 minutes
Cooking time 35 minutes
Level easy
Wine medium-structured red with bouquet of ripe red fruits and herbs,
such as Trentino Marzemino

Rinse the lentils under running water and soak them in cold water for about 2 hours.

Heat the olive oil with the garlic and sauté the minced celery, carrot, and onion until soft. Add the lentils, curry, and tomato paste. Sauté for a few minutes, then add the hot broth and cook for 30 minutes until the lentils are soft and the liquid has evaporated.

Puree the lentil mixture in a food processor until smooth, then season to taste with salt and pepper. Stir in the parsley.

Divide the pâté between individual ramekins and let cool to room temperature before serving.

Cook's tip The pâté can be garnished with a few whole chervil or parsley leaves and served with toasted bread.

Coppa and Artichoke Canapés

Serves 8

12 slices of rye bread
7 ounces fresh goat's milk cheese
5½ ounces coppa, thinly sliced
7 ounces baby artichokes in oil, drained and sliced
salt and pepper

Preparation time 10 minutes
Level easy
Wine Charmat method, fresh and light-bodied sparkling wine,
such as Prosecco di Valdobbiadene Extra Dry

Spread half the slices of bread with goat's cheese. Top them with the coppa and artichokes, season with salt and pepper, then close with the remaining slices of bread.

Wrap the sandwiches in plastic wrap and refrigerate for about 1 hour. Unwrap the sandwiches, slice into small triangles or rectangles, fix with toothpicks, and serve.

Cook's tip The coppa can be replaced with smoked ham or prosciutto.

Mortadella Canapés

Serves 4

3½ ounces gherkins, plus extra for garnish
10½ ounces ricotta
1 tarragon sprig, minced
salt
12 large slices of mortadella
sun-dried cherry tomatoes, halved

Preparation time 15 minutes
Level easy
Wine sparkling, light-bodied red with delicate bouquet of fresh red fruits,
such as Emilia-Romagna Lambrusco

Drain the gherkins and finely mince them. Stir together the ricotta, gherkins, and tarragon. Salt to taste.

Lay three slices of mortadella on a work surface. Spread each one with the ricotta mixture and cover with another slice of mortadella. Continue making layers, finishing with a slice of mortadella. Wrap in plastic wrap and refrigerate for about an hour.

Unwrap, cut into wedges, and serve, garnished with gherkins and sun-dried cherry tomato halves and skewered with a toothpick.

Cook's tip For an even more flavorful variation, replace the ricotta and gherkin mixture with 9 ounces Gorgonzola cheese, beaten until smooth.

Potato and Arugula Terrine

Serves 4

4 large yellow-fleshed potatoes
4 tablespoons extra-virgin olive oil
1 shallot, chopped
1 thyme sprig, chopped
3 ounces prosciutto, diced
salt and pepper
1 bunch arugula, chopped
1 garlic clove
2 slices crusty bread

Preparation time 30 minutes
Cooking time 30 minutes
Level easy
Wine well-structured white with body and evolved bouquet of ripe fruit,
such as Friuli Malvasia Istriana

Place the unpeeled potatoes in a large saucepan of cold, salted water. Boil the potatoes until tender. Let cool slightly, then peel and mash.

Heat 2 tablespoons of the olive oil in a large saucepan and add the shallot. When the shallot begins to brown, add the mashed potatoes, thyme, and prosciutto. Cook over medium heat for 5 minutes.

Remove from heat, let cool slightly, and season to taste with salt and pepper. Stir in the arugula and transfer the mixture to a rectangular mold or terrine pan lined with plastic wrap. Refrigerate for 1 hour.

Brown the garlic clove in the remaining olive oil in a nonstick frying pan. Remove the garlic clove and add the bread slices. Fry until golden brown. Chop or crumble the fried bread to make breadcrumbs.

Unmold the terrine and sprinkle with the garlic-flavored breadcrumbs. Slice and serve immediately.

Mortadella and Pistachio Terrine

Serves 4

2 slices of white bread
14 ounces mortadella, diced
½ cup (1 stick) butter, softened
3 ½ ounces mascarpone
salt and pepper
⅓ cup (1 ½ ounces) shelled pistachios, peeled

Preparation time 10 minutes
Level easy
Wine young, light-bodied, fresh and fragrant red,
such as Emilia-Romagna Colli Bolognesi Merlot

Blend the bread in a food processor, then add the mortadella and continue blending until the mixture is smooth.

Transfer to bowl and mix in the softened butter, then the mascarpone, and beat until smooth. Season with salt and pepper.

Chop half the pistachios and stir them into the mortadella mixture.

Line a small terrine mold with parchment paper. Sprinkle the remaining pistachios in the bottom and then fill with the mortadella mixture. Level off the top and refrigerate for a few hours. Unmold the terrine and serve sliced.

Cook's tip Serve the terrine with toasted slices of rye bread or slices of baguette.

Ricotta-Stuffed Phyllo with Tomato Salad

Serves 4

Phyllo parcels
1 cup (7 ounces) sheep's-milk ricotta (or cow's-milk ricotta that has been drained overnight)
1 tablespoon grated Pecorino Romano cheese
2 thyme sprigs, leaves only
freshly ground black pepper
4 sheets of phyllo dough
sunflower oil for frying

Tomato salad
2 plum tomatoes, diced
1 garlic clove, minced
2 tablespoons extra-virgin olive oil
salt and pepper

Preparation time 20 minutes
Cooking time 5 minutes
Level easy
Wine medium-bodied white with bouquet of ripe yellow fruit,
such as Sicily Bianco d'Alcamo

Mix the ricotta, grated Pecorino Romano, and thyme leaves until smooth. Add the pepper.

Separate the phyllo sheets and cut them into 3-inch-wide strips. Starting from the outside edge of each strip, place a spoonful of the ricotta mixture on the dough and fold over 3 times, making little parcels. Repeat for each strip, using all of the ricotta mixture.

Toss the tomatoes with garlic, olive oil, salt, and pepper. Let sit for 10 minutes.

Heat the sunflower oil and fry the parcels until golden and crispy. Serve hot, accompanied by the tomato salad.

Variation The phyllo dough could be replaced by a dough made from ¾ cup (3½ ounces) all-purpose flour and ¾ cup (3½ ounces) farro (emmer wheat) flour. Mix in pinches of salt and pepper, 1 tablespoon extra-virgin olive oil, and enough lukewarm water to make a smooth dough. Knead well then let rest. Roll out thinly and then proceed as above.

Chickpea and Eggplant Dip

Serves 4

Dip
1 cup (7 ounces) dried chickpeas
1 bay leaf
1 garlic clove
2 large eggplants
3 tablespoons extra-virgin olive oil
1 tablespoon sesame oil
1 bunch of parsley, stemmed and minced
salt and pepper

Garnish
1 red bell pepper
1 yellow bell pepper

Toast
4 slices of bread

Preparation time 15 minutes
Cooking time 120 minutes
Level easy
Wine white with well-structured body, rich in yellow fruit fragrances,
such as Campania Greco di Tufo

Soak the chickpeas in cold water for 12 hours.
Drain the chickpeas and boil them with the bay leaf and garlic clove until tender.
Preheat oven to 350°F.
Cut the eggplant in half lengthwise and score the flesh with a sharp knife to create many parallel cuts. Bake in the oven for about 30 minutes until soft. Scoop out the pulp with a spoon and puree it with the cooked chickpeas (reserve a few whole chickpeas for garnish). Pass the mixture through a sieve, then stir in the olive oil, sesame oil, parsley, salt, and pepper. Keep cool.
Roast the peppers over an open flame or under a broiler. Put them in a plastic bag, close it, and let steam for 20 minutes. Peel, seed, and wash the peppers, then cut into julienne strips.
Toast the bread in a nonstick frying pan or under the broiler.
Transfer the dip to small bowls. Garnish with the roasted peppers and a few whole chickpeas and serve with the toasts immediately.

Steamed Eggs with Salsa Verde

Serves 4

Eggs
4 large fresh eggs

Salsa verde
1 large fresh egg
1 tablespoon pine nuts
1 bunch of basil
parsley
6 tablespoons extra-virgin olive oil
salt and pepper

Garnish (optional)
½ black truffle

Preparation time 10 minutes
Cooking time 15 minutes
Level easy
Wine young red without overly pronounced structure, such as Alto Adige Pinot Noir

FRESH EGGS
A way of testing the freshness of eggs is to see whether they sink or float: immerse an egg in a glass of salted water (1 tablespoon salt per cup water). If it sinks, the egg is very fresh; if it stays halfway, it is up to 6 days old; if it bobs to the surface, it is up to 11 days old, and if it floats, it is probably rotten and should be thrown out.

Crack 4 eggs into 4 coffee cups. Cover with plastic wrap and set aside.

Boil the remaining egg until hard. Drain, cool, and peel off the shell. Separate the yolk and the white.

Toast the pine nuts in a nonstick pan.

Put the basil, parsley, and pine nuts in a food processor with the hard-boiled egg white, olive oil, and salt and pepper. Puree until creamy.

Heat a little water in a saucepan and when it boils, place a steamer basket on top. Place the coffee cups with the eggs in the basket and cook for about 9 minutes, until the egg white is firm.

Run a thin knife around the eggs to loosen them from the cups, then place the eggs onto plates with the salsa verde. Garnish with truffle shavings.

Crispy Polenta with Pea Puree

Serves 4

Polenta
1 ¼ cups water
sea salt
¾ cup (3 ½ ounces) instant polenta
sunflower oil for frying

Pea puree
2 tablespoons extra-virgin olive oil
1 shallot, minced
½ chili pepper
1 cup (7 ounces) fresh peas
½ cup vegetable broth
salt and pepper
chives, minced

Preparation time 20 minutes
Cooking time 35 minutes
Level easy
Wine young red with bouquet of fresh red fruits,
such as Friuli Merlot

Bring the water to a boil with a pinch of sea salt, then gradually whisk in the polenta. Let thicken, then pour into a square mold and let cool.

Heat the olive oil in a frying pan and sauté the shallot and chili pepper over low heat. Add the peas and broth. Cook until tender, then season to taste with salt and pepper and puree in a food processor. Stir in the chives.

Cut the polenta into rectangles. Heat the sunflower oil and fry the polenta until crispy. Drain and dry on paper towels, then serve topped with the pea puree.

Savory Parmesan Baskets

Serves 4

4 tablespoons grated Parmesan cheese
1 strip of roasted red bell pepper
1 strip of roasted yellow bell pepper
2 tablespoons butter
½ Golden Delicious apple, cut into ½-inch cubes
salt and pepper
2 teaspoons fresh goat cheese
2 anchovy fillets in oil
chives, minced

Preparation time 15 minutes
Cooking time 20 minutes
Level medium
Wine white with well-structured body and very intense, persistent fragrances, such as Sicily Chardonnay Barrique

Heat a small nonstick frying pan and place a round cookie cutter (1½ inches in diameter) in the middle. Sprinkle a tablespoon of Parmesan inside the cutter. Once it melts, remove the cutter. When the cheese is browned, remove from the pan and carefully arrange over an upside-down espresso coffee cup or shot glass. Repeat three more times, to make four Parmesan baskets. Let cool over the cups.

Meanwhile peel the peppers (if necessary) and cut into thinner strips.

Heat the butter in a frying pan and sauté the apple with salt and pepper.

Place the Parmesan baskets on plates and place an apple cube in the center of each. Lay pepper strips around the apple, then top with goat cheese and finish with a piece of anchovy fillet. Sprinkle with chives and serve.

Truffled Mushroom Pâté

Serves 4

Pâté
3 tablespoons extra-virgin olive oil
2 garlic cloves, smashed
1 small onion, thinly sliced
1 pound 2 ounces mixed mushrooms (such as button, porcini, chanterelles), sliced
salt and pepper
½ cup fresh cream
½ cup (3½ ounces) truffle butter, melted
1 bunch of mixed herbs (thyme, marjoram, chives), minced

Garnish
1 baguette

Preparation time 15 minutes
Cooking time 25 minutes
Level easy
Wine young red with grassy, red-fruit aromas, such as Piedmont Barbera

Heat the olive oil in a frying pan with the garlic and sauté the onion. Add the mushrooms and sauté for 15 to 20 minutes, stirring frequently. Season to taste with salt and pepper, then remove and discard the garlic. Let cool slightly, then puree the mixture in a food processor with the cream and melted truffle butter. Stir in the minced herbs, salt, and pepper, then transfer to a bowl or individual serving dishes. Refrigerate until firm.

Meanwhile slice and toast the baguette. Serve the pâté with the pieces of toast. The pâté can also be shaped like quenelles using two spoons, then arranged on a plate.

Cook's tip To preserve aromatic herbs, follow this procedure: chop the herbs, keeping the different types separate (photo 1); put them in an ice-cube tray, adding a little water (photo 2). Freeze them until solid, then remove from tray and wrap each kind separately in aluminum foil (photo 3), labeling each with a felt-tip pen. Store in the freezer until needed.

1   2   3

Vegetables with Yogurt Mayonnaise

Serves 6

Vegetables
3 carrots, peeled and diced
2 yellow-fleshed potatoes, peeled and diced
2 zucchini, diced
2 cooked beets, peeled and diced

Yogurt mayonnaise
1 egg yolk
salt
1 pinch mild mustard powder
1 container plain yogurt (4 ounces)
1 teaspoon lemon juice
½ cup corn oil
1 teaspoon chives, minced

Preparation time 30 minutes
Cooking time 15 minutes
Level easy
Wine no wine recommended

Steam the carrots, potatoes, and zucchini separately until tender.

Whisk the egg yolk with some salt, the mustard, and lemon juice. Continue mixing (either with a whisk or with an electric beater), adding the corn oil drop by drop, and then in a thin stream. Mix in the yogurt and chives. Refrigerate for at least 2 hours before serving.

Serve the beets and the other vegetables with the yogurt mayonnaise.

Cook's tip Yogurt mayonnaise makes a good dressing for seasonal summer salads.

Stuffed Zucchini with Crispy Zucchini Flowers

Serves 4

Stuffed zucchini
2 tablespoons extra-virgin olive oil
2 garlic cloves, smashed
1 pinch chili pepper flakes
4 large zucchini
6 capers
10 black olives, pitted
1 bunch of basil, torn into pieces
2 tablespoons breadcrumbs
1 egg

Zucchini flowers
sunflower oil for frying
very cold sparkling water
¼ cup (2 ounces) all-purpose flour
1 tablespoon poppy seeds
salt
8 zucchini flowers, pistils removed

Preparation time 25 minutes
Cooking time 25 minutes
Level easy
Wine medium-bodied white with fragrant aromas of yellow fruits,
such as Sicily Bianco d'Alcamo

Preheat oven to 350°F.

Place the olive oil in a large frying pan with the garlic and chili pepper flakes and let sit. Remove the ends of the zucchini, then use an apple corer to remove the seedy inner flesh.

Dice the zucchini flesh and add to the frying pan. Add the capers, olives, and basil and sauté on high heat for 10 minutes. Add a little water if necessary. Remove the garlic and puree the rest of the mixture in a food processor with the breadcrumbs and egg.

Steam the hollowed-out zucchini for 5 minutes, then stuff with the filling. Bake for 10 minutes.

Meanwhile heat the sunflower oil. Whisk the cold sparkling water into the flour, adding the poppy seeds and a pinch of salt. Dip the zucchini flowers into the batter, shake to remove excess batter, then fry in the hot sunflower oil until golden. Drain and pat dry on paper towels.

Serve the stuffed zucchini with the crispy flowers immediately.

Cook's tip To get a crispier fry, use very cold beer instead of sparkling water.

Phyllo Cups with Artichoke Pâté

Serves 4

4 sheets phyllo dough
2 tablespoons butter
4 artichokes
juice and zest of 1 lemon
3 tablespoons extra-virgin olive oil
1 shallot, diced
1 small mild red chili pepper, minced
½ cup vegetable broth
parsley, chopped
⅓ cup (1½ ounces) peanuts, chopped
salt and pepper
1 bunch chives, chopped

Preparation time 30 minutes
Cooking time 30 minutes
Level medium
Wine white with well-structured body and aromatic bouquet,
such as Alto Adige Riesling Renano

Preheat oven to 400°F.
   Roll out the phyllo dough on a work surface, without separating the sheets of dough. Using a large circular cookie cutter, cut out 8 rounds of dough. Press the dough over 8 buttered, ovenproof ramekins and bake for 5 minutes. Remove from the oven and let cool.
   Remove the tough outer leaves and choke from the artichokes. Soak for 5 minutes in water acidulated with lemon juice. Drain and thinly slice the artichokes.
   Heat the olive oil in a large frying pan, add the shallot and chili pepper, and brown slightly. Add the artichokes and vegetable broth. Reduce the heat and simmer until the artichokes are just tender. Add the parsley, half of the peanuts, and the lemon zest. Remove from heat and season to taste with salt and pepper.
   Puree the mixture and transfer to a pastry bag. Pipe the puree into the phyllo cups. Garnish with the remaining peanuts and the chives.

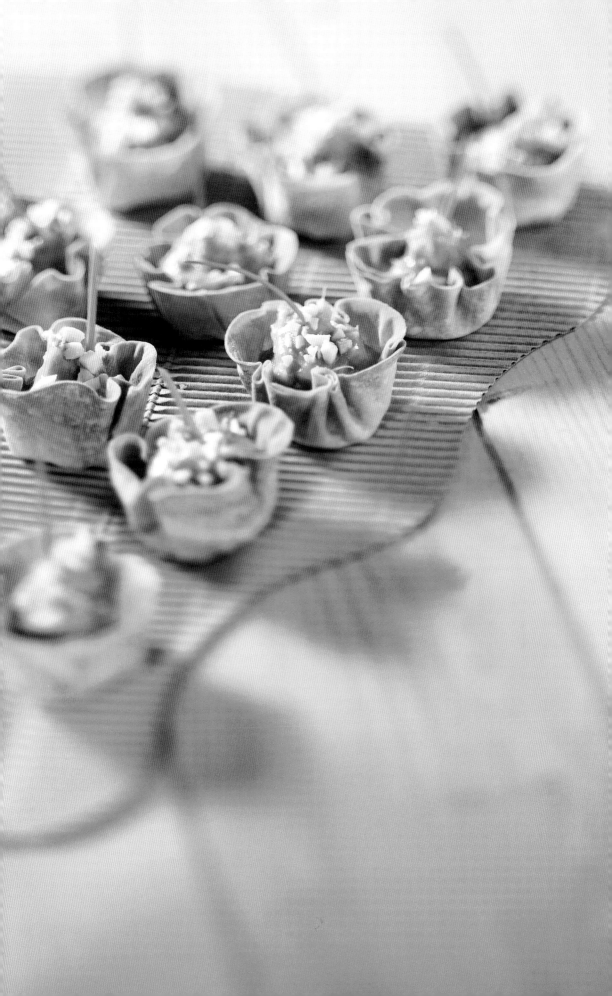

Herbed Cheese with Tomatoes and Olives

Serves 4

1 pound robiola or other soft, fresh cheese
1 cup (1 ounce) minced fresh herbs (basil, chives, parsley, thyme),
   plus extra for garnish
4 tablespoons extra-virgin olive oil
salt and pepper
2 cups (9 ounces) cherry tomatoes, quartered
½ cup (2 ounces) pitted black olives
bread, toasted

Preparation time 20 minutes
Level easy
Wine white with well-structured body and intense aromas of yellow fruit,
such as Campania Fiano di Avellino

Mix together the robiola, minced herbs, and 2 tablespoons olive oil. Season with salt and pepper.

Line four small dome molds with plastic wrap and fill them with the cheese mixture. Refrigerate until time to serve.

Drain the tomatoes in a colander, then transfer to a bowl and mix with the olives and a little salt.

Unmold the cheese domes and garnish with the tomatoes and olives. Drizzle with the remaining olive oil. Garnish with fresh herbs and serve with toasted bread.

Avocado Salad with Pancetta and Spring Onions

Serves 4

2 avocados
juice of 1 lemon
4 ounces pancetta or bacon, thickly sliced
2 spring onions, thinly sliced
4 tablespoons extra-virgin olive oil
salt and pepper
corn chips

Preparation time 15 minutes
Cooking time 2 minutes
Level easy
Wine Charmat method, fresh and light-bodied sparkling wine,
such as Prosecco di Valdobbiadene Brut

Preheat the oven to 400°F.
   Halve the avocados, remove the pit, then peel and dice them. Toss with the lemon juice.
   Lay the pancetta or bacon slices on a baking tray and toast in the oven for a few minutes until crispy. Alternatively, crisp the slices in a hot frying pan. Drain off the fat and let them cool.
   Stir the spring onions into the avocado and dress with olive oil, salt, and pepper. Break the pancetta or bacon into pieces and add to the salad. Serve with corn chips.

Cook's tip Try adding thinly sliced Belgian endive or radicchio to the salad. As an alternative to corn chips, serve with croutons of toasted bread.

Stuffed Leeks with Arugula Salad

Serves 4

Leeks
2 large leeks
extra-virgin olive oil
2 white onions, peeled and sliced
11 ounces fresh goat cheese

Salad
2 tomatoes, diced
2 bunches of arugula, chopped
1 tablespoon pine nuts
1 tablespoon capers, chopped
extra-virgin olive oil
salt and pepper
toasted sesame seeds

Preparation time 25 minutes
Cooking time 15 minutes
Level easy
Wine Dry white with well-structured body and evolved bouquet of yellow fruits, such as Campania Falanghina Barrique

LEEKS
These are a common winter vegetable. Choose very fresh and pale leeks. White leeks are tenderer and more delicate in flavor. The white stalk is generally used more in cooking than the green leaves.

Remove the green part of the leeks and cut off the roots. Cut each leek in half lengthwise, then carefully remove the inner part to create four "boats." Blanch in boiling water for 30 seconds, then drain and let cool.

Heat a drizzle of oil in a frying pan and sauté the sliced onions until translucent, adding water if necessary. Remove from the heat and let cool slightly, then stir in the cheese. (If the mixture is too soft, add some grated Parmesan and/or breadcrumbs.) Transfer the mixture to a pastry bag.

Fill the leek boats with the onion-cheese mixture, then wrap in plastic wrap and refrigerate.

Toss the tomatoes, arugula, pine nuts, and capers with a drizzle of olive oil, salt, and pepper. Divide the salad between plates and top with the filled leeks. Garnish with toasted sesame seeds.

Caprese

Serves 4

5 tomatoes, sliced
1 pound 2 ounces buffalo mozzarella, sliced
4 tablespoons extra-virgin olive oil
salt
oregano
basil leaves

Preparation time 10 minutes
Level easy
Wine medium-bodied white with fresh and fragrant bouquet,
such as Campania Capri Bianco

Arrange the tomato and mozzarella slices on a serving plate. Season with olive oil, a pinch of salt and a generous sprinkling of oregano. Garnish with fresh basil leaves.

Variation Cow's-milk mozzarella, known in Italy as fior di latte, can be used instead of buffalo mozzarella.

Fish and Shellfish

Sea bass, tuna, salmon, and shellfish
are featured in these delicate and
original appetizers. Start your meals
with flavor and imagination.

Cockle-Stuffed Sea Bass with Vegetables

Serves 4

Sea bass
10 fresh cockles, washed
2 garlic cloves, smashed
1 dried chili pepper
2 tablespoons extra-virgin olive oil
salt and pepper
4 sea bass fillets (about 4½ ounces each)
basil

Vegetables
sunflower oil for frying
1 small eggplant, washed and diced
2 zucchini, washed and diced
1 tablespoon extra-virgin olive oil
thyme
salt

Lentil puree
¼ cup (2¼ ounces) red lentils
¾ cup vegetable stock
1 fresh chili pepper, salt
3 tablespoons extra-virgin olive oil

Preparation time 25 minutes
Cooking time 1 hour 10 minutes
Level medium
Wine young, medium-bodied white with fragrant, grassy, yellow-fruit bouquet,
such as Tuscany Elba Bianco

Place the cockles, garlic, dried chili pepper, and olive oil in a saucepan. Cover and cook over high heat until the cockles open; season to taste with salt and pepper.

Cut the sea bass fillets in half lengthwise and place each piece between 2 oiled sheets of plastic wrap. Pound lightly with a meat tenderizer. Remove cockles from their shells and place a few in the center of each fillet. Top each fillet with a basil leaf and roll up carefully. Wrap the fillets in plastic warp and twist the ends like a candy wrapper. Heat the sunflower oil in a large frying pan, add the diced eggplant and zucchini, and fry until golden brown. Remove from the oil using a slotted spoon and drain on paper towels. Transfer the vegetables to another frying pan and sauté with the olive oil and some thyme. Season to taste with salt.

Boil the lentils in the stock with a small piece of the fresh chili pepper until soft, adding more stock or water if necessary. Puree the lentils, then pass through a sieve. Season to taste with salt and drizzle with olive oil. Steam the fish parcels until tender. Remove the plastic wrap and serve with the vegetables and lentil puree.

Catalan-Style Langoustines with Vegetables

Serves 4

Court bouillon
1 shallot, chopped
1 celery stalk, washed and chopped
1 bay leaf
1 carrot, peeled and chopped
1 parsley sprig
white wine
black pepper

Langoustines
16 medium-small langoustines
1 bunch celery, tender heart only, thinly sliced
2 small carrots, peeled and julienned
1 cucumber, peeled, seeded, and julienned

Vinaigrette
3 tablespoons balsamic vinegar
salt and white pepper
4 tablespoons extra-virgin olive oil

Preparation time 15 minutes
Cooking time 25 minutes
Level easy
Wine medium-bodied white with intense aromas of yellow fruits and spices,
such as Sicily Inzolia

Place all of the ingredients for the court boullion in a large pot of water and bring to a boil. Simmer until the vegetables are just tender, then use the broth to blanch the langoustines for 4 minutes. Using a slotted spoon, remove the langoustines and peel them.

Make small nests with the sliced celery heart and the julienned carrots and cucumber in small glass bowls or on individual serving plates. Top with the peeled langoustines.

Dissolve the salt in the vinegar and whisk in the olive oil. Season the vinaigrette with a pinch of white pepper and drizzle over the langoustines and vegetables.

Cook's tip For a more exotic dish, try adding a few pineapple slices and strawberries or some slices of white melon to the julienned vegetables. For a richer variation, add prawns or lobsters to the scampi.

Zucchini Rolls with Tuna and Capers

Serves 4

Zucchini
3 large zucchini, trimmed and sliced lengthwise
6½ ounces tuna in oil
1 spring onion, minced
1 tablespoon extra-virgin olive oil
6 pitted green and black olives, coarsely chopped
8 capers, rinsed and coarsely chopped
salt and pepper
1 leek, cut into thin strips

Garnish
5 fresh basil leaves

Preparation time 20 minutes
Cooking time 15 minutes
Level easy
Wine young, light-bodied white with herbaceous bouquet,
such as Veneto Gambellara

Heat a cast-iron grill pan over high heat and grill the zucchini slices. Remove from heat and set aside.

Drain the tuna and puree it with the spring onion and olive oil in a food processor. Stir in the olives and capers and season to taste with salt and pepper.

Place 1 tablespoon of filling in the center of each zucchini slice and roll up.

Blanch the leek strips in salted boiling water for 1 minute. Remove and pat dry. Tie up each zucchini roll using a leek strip and garnish with basil.

Refrigerate the zucchini rolls for at least 30 minutes before serving.

Cook's tip For a vegetarian version of this recipe, replace the tuna with 7 ounces fresh tofu, boiled in hot water for 7 minutes.

Scallops and Porcini with Mint

Serves 4

4 large scallops in the shell
2 small porcini mushrooms
salt
white and black pepper
2 tablespoons delicate extra-virgin olive oil
2 mint sprigs, minced
1 ½ teaspoons fine breadcrumbs

Preparation time 20 minutes
Cooking time 1 minute
Level easy
Wine young light-bodied and unstructured red,
such as Veneto Piave Merlot

Preheat the broiler.

Remove the scallops from their shells and carefully wash them. Thinly slice the scallops on the diagonal using a sharp knife. Wash the shells and set them aside (they can be used as serving dishes).

Cut away the earthy bottom of the mushroom stems, and clean the mushroom tops and stems using a damp paper towel. Thinly slice the mushrooms, taking care not to break the slices, and set them aside.

Alternate the scallop slices and porcini mushrooms in the shells. Season with salt and white and black pepper, and drizzle with the extra-virgin olive oil. Top with mint and sprinkle with a pinch of breadcrumbs. Broil the shells for 1 minute and serve immediately. If desired, you can decorate the scallops with cherry tomatoes.

Cook's tip This dish is even better with the herb Italians call nepitella (lesser calamint), which has a lighter and more delicate fragrance than common mint.

Sole and Salmon Rolls

Serves 4

Rolls
8 sole fillets
3 ½ ounces fresh salmon fillet, thinly sliced
1 cup (3 ½ ounces) fresh spinach, washed and stems trimmed
salt and pepper
extra-virgin olive oil

Salad
2 bunches spinach
8 quail eggs
4 tomatoes, peeled, seeded, and diced
1 cucumber, peeled and diced
extra-virgin olive oil

Marinated bread
11 ounces Tuscan-style bread
salt and pepper
6 tablespoons extra-virgin olive oil
4 salted anchovies, chopped
2 tablespoons red wine vinegar

Preparation time 40 minutes
Cooking time 15 minutes
Level medium
Wine well-structured white with an aromatic bouquet,
such as Friuli Collio Sauvignon

Gently flatten out the sole fillets using a meat tenderizer. Arrange the salmon slices on top of the sole fillets. Place the spinach leaves over the salmon. Roll up the fillets and let sit in the refrigerator for 5 minutes.

Meanwhile wash the spinach for the salad and blanch in boiling water for 1 minute; drain and let cool in cold water.

Boil the quail eggs for 1 minute, then drain and immediately immerse in cold water. Shell the eggs, taking care not to break them. Cut the bread into very thin slices, dice, and spread out on a baking sheet. Season with pinches of salt and pepper and drizzle with olive oil. Sprinkle with the chopped anchovies, add the vinegar, and let sit for at least 5 minutes.

Season the fish rolls with salt and pepper and drizzle with olive oil. Steam the rolls for 3 minutes. Drain the spinach and steam for 3 minutes.

Place the blanched spinach on individual serving plates and put the sole rolls on top. Place the quail eggs between the sole rolls, then sprinkle with the diced tomatoes and cucumber. Top with the marinated bread and drizzle with extra-virgin olive oil. Serve immediately.

Polenta Squares with Spicy Baby Octopus

Serves 4

Polenta squares
2 cups water
salt
1 cup (5 ounces) instant polenta
sunflower oil for frying

Baby octopus
9 ounces baby octopus, rinsed and cleaned
3 tablespoons extra-virgin olive oil
2 garlic cloves, halved
1 chili pepper
½ cup white wine
parsley, chopped
10 ripe cherry tomatoes, sliced (or crushed canned tomatoes)
salt and pepper

Preparation time 20 minutes
Cooking time 30 minutes
Level easy
Wine young, light-bodied red with a fresh bouquet,
such as Alto Adige Cabernet Sauvignon

Salt the water, bring to a boil, and slowly whisk in the polenta. Continue stirring with a wooden spoon for 5 minutes. Line a terrine dish or loaf pan with plastic wrap, and add the polenta. Refrigerate until firm.

Roughly chop the octopus and rinse.

Heat the olive oil in a large frying pan. Add the garlic and chili pepper, and sauté briefly. Add the octopus and brown for 1 minute, then pour in the wine. Add the parsley and tomatoes. Cook over low heat for about 15 minutes. Season to taste with salt and pepper.

Unmold the polenta and cut into slices. Fry the polenta in the sunflower oil until golden brown, drain, and dry on paper towels. Top the crunchy polenta squares with the octopus ragù and serve immediately.

Cook's tip The octopus ragù must be quite thick so that it stays on top of the polenta squares instead of making them soggy.

Baby Squid with Squid-Ink Potatoes

Serves 4

extra-virgin olive oil
1 cup (5½ ounces) diced onion
40 very small baby squid
1 cup (3½ ounces) thinly sliced leeks
1 large potato, peeled and chopped
basil leaves
1 marjoram sprig
½ cup langoustine, lobster, and/or shrimp bisque
1¼ cups fish broth
salt and pepper
4 to 5 squid-ink sacs (nero di seppie)
1 tablespoon white wine vinegar
4 quail eggs
1 summer truffle, shaved (optional)

Preparation time 30 minutes
Cooking time 25 minutes
Level medium
Wine well-structured white with a pronounced aromas,
such as Sicily Inzolia Barrique

Preheat oven to 425°F.
   Heat a drizzle of olive oil in a frying pan and sauté the onion until soft.
   Clean and wash the squid and dry them with a paper towel. Detach and set aside the heads, and stuff the bodies with the sautéed onion.
   Heat another drizzle of olive oil in a large frying pan, add the leeks, and sauté briefly. Add the potato, basil, and marjoram. Sauté for a few minutes, then add the bisque and fish broth and cook over low heat for 15 minutes. Season with salt and pepper, then puree the sauce, adding 1 tablespoon of extra-virgin olive oil and the squid ink. Set aside in a warm place.
   Place the stuffed squid on a baking sheet, sprinkle with salt and pepper, and drizzle with olive oil. Bake in oven for 10 minutes.
   Meanwhile bring a pot of lightly salted water to a boil. Add the white wine vinegar and stir with a wooden spoon to create a whirlpool. Break in the quail eggs. As soon as they are cooked on the outside, drain and place in a bowl of cold water.
   Sauté the squid heads in a pan with a drizzle of oil until cooked through.
   Pour a spoonful of potato sauce into 4 soup bowls and arrange 10 squid in a ring in each bowl; in the middle of this ring place 10 squid heads, and a quail egg, then drizzle with olive oil and sprinkle with truffle shavings.

Tuna Mille-feuille

Serves 4

2 sheets frozen phyllo dough
2 tablespoons butter, melted
salt and pepper
4 tablespoons extra-virgin olive oil
1 garlic clove, smashed
1 cup (5 ounces) green beans, blanched
1 rosemary sprig
½ cup vegetable broth
7 ounces tuna in oil

Preparation time 20 minutes
Cooking time 10 minutes
Level easy
Wine well-structured white with elegant notes of fruit,
such as Campania Falanghina

Preheat oven to 375°F.

Cut phyllo pastry into 1½-inch squares. Lay the squares on a parchment paper-lined baking sheet. Brush each square with melted butter and sprinkle with salt and pepper. Bake for about 6 minutes, until golden brown.

Heat the olive oil in a saucepan with the garlic clove. Add the beans and rosemary and sauté briefly. Remove the garlic and rosemary, and season to taste with salt and pepper. Pour in the broth and continue cooking for 5 minutes. Drain the beans, reserving the stock, and set aside.

Puree the tuna with 2 tablespoons of the beans and the reserved cooking liquid in a blender or food processor. Transfer the puree to a bowl and set aside.

Puree the remaining beans into a smooth, rather liquid consistency, adding more broth if necessary. Pass the puree through a wide-mesh sieve.

Make alternating layers of phyllo squares and tuna puree on individual serving plates to create mille-feuilles. Place a few spoonfuls of bean puree around the mille-feuilles and drizzle with olive oil.

Variation Fresh tuna can be used instead of the tuna in oil. Chop 12 ounces of fresh tuna and sauté in a nonstick pan with a little oil, 1 smashed garlic clove, thyme, salt, and pepper. Thinly slice the cooked fish and compose the mille-feuilles by alternating the crispy phyllo squares, bean puree, and tuna slices on serving plates.

Scallops and Brussels Sprouts with White Polenta

Serves 4

Scallops and brussels sprouts
4 shallots
1 thyme sprig
12 small scallops
extra-virgin olive oil
16 brussels sprouts
salt and pepper

Polenta
2 cups fish broth
¾ cup (3 ounces) white cornmeal
1 thyme sprig
3 tablespoons extra-virgin olive oil
1 tablespoon butter
salt and pepper

Preparation time 30 minutes
Cooking time 45 minutes
Level easy
Wine medium-bodied, fresh white with herbaceous notes,
such as Alto Adige Sauvignon

Preheat oven to 400°F.

Wrap the unpeeled shallots and the sprig of thyme in aluminum foil. Bake for about 25 minutes, remove from the oven, and let cool slightly in the foil.

Meanwhile, remove the scallops from their shells and wash thoroughly. Drizzle the scallops with olive oil, cover with plastic wrap, and refrigerate.

Cut off and discard the outer leaves and hard stalk of the brussels sprouts, then steam the vegetables for 6 to 7 minutes. Remove from the heat and cut into quarters.

Strain the fish broth and bring it to a boil in a heavy-bottomed saucepan. Pour in the polenta in a thin stream, whisking constantly. Cook over low heat, stirring continuously with a wooden spoon, until the polenta is soft and creamy. Stir in the thyme leaves, olive oil, and butter and season with salt and pepper.

Heat a nonstick pan and briefly sauté the scallops until just barely cooked through. Remove from heat and season with salt and pepper.

Spread a layer of polenta on each serving plate, top with the quartered brussels sprouts, and then add another layer of soft polenta. Top with hot scallops and serve with the roasted shallots.

Baby Squid with Bell Peppers and Onions

Serves 4

Squid
20 small baby squid
1 red bell pepper
1 yellow bell pepper
1 green bell pepper
2 tablespoons extra-virgin olive oil
spice rub for grilled fish

Onions
4 tablespoons extra-virgin olive oil
20 pearl onions, peeled
1 tablespoon sugar
4 tablespoons balsamic vinegar

Potatoes
2 tablespoons extra-virgin olive oil
2 new potatoes, peeled and diced
fresh rosemary and thyme
salt and pepper

Preparation time 30 minutes
Cooking time 25 minutes
Level medium
Wine medium-bodied white with an intense and persistent bouquet,
such as Sardinia Vermentino di Gallura

Preheat oven to 400°F.

Clean the squid.

Cut the peppers into strips ¾-inch longer than the squid. Stuff the squid with the peppers and let marinate for 10 minutes in the olive oil with the spice rub. Place the stuffed squid on a baking sheet and bake for 10 minutes.

Make the onions: Heat the olive oil in a frying pan and add the onions. Sprinkle with the sugar and let caramelize. When the onions begin to brown, pour in the balsamic vinegar and let reduce. Continue cooking the onions until tender, adding a little water if necessary.

Make the potatoes: Heat the olive oil in a large frying pan over high heat. Add the potatoes, rosemary, and thyme. Pan-fry the potatoes until tender and season to taste with salt and pepper.

Arrange the potatoes on plates, top with the stuffed squid, and add the caramelized onions.

Zucchini Rings with Squid

ZUCCHINI

A nutritious vegetable, zucchini is low in calories and rich in vitamins A and C, as well as such minerals as iron and phosphorus. While zucchini is traditionally a spring crop, it is now readily available year-round. When buying zucchini, make sure that the vegetable is firm and the skin is unmarked.

Serves 4

½ red bell pepper
½ yellow bell pepper
7 to 8 small zucchini with flowers
6 tablespoons extra-virgin olive oil
2 slices of soft bread
½ cup milk
salt and pepper
20 baby squid, cleaned
sunflower oil for frying

Preparation time 35 minutes
Cooking time 20 minutes
Level medium
Wine well-structured white with persistent
flavors, such as Friuli Malvasia Istriana

Roast the peppers under a broiler or over an open flame. Close them in a plastic bag for at least 15 minutes to steam. Peel, seed, and set aside.

Meanwhile trim the zucchini, reserving the flowers. Slice the zucchini very thinly lengthwise using a mandoline. Steam the zucchini strips for 1 minute.

Lightly oil four individual ring molds and line them with the zucchini slices.

Soak the bread slices in the milk until soft, drain, and squeeze out the excess liquid. Crumble the bread into a bowl and season with salt and pepper.

Slice a few strips of each pepper and set aside. Dice the remaining pepper and combine with the bread; mix well. Fill the lined molds with the bread and pepper mixture, and fold the zucchini slices over the top. Steam the molds for a few minutes, to heat through.

Meanwhile blanch the baby squid in salted water and fry the zucchini flowers in hot sunflower oil until crispy.

Remove the zucchini rings from the molds, transfer onto individual serving plates, and place the baby squid in the center of the rings. Garnish with pepper strips and a drizzle of olive oil. Serve with the fried zucchini flowers.

Cod and Potato Puree with Peach Sauce

Serves 4

Cod and potato puree
2 tablespoons extra-virgin olive oil
1 shallot, minced
5 ounces salt cod, soaked and rinsed
9 ounces yellow-fleshed potatoes, thinly sliced
¾ cup milk
parsley, chopped
salt and pepper

Peach sauce
2 yellow peaches, peeled and diced
juice from ½ lemon
½ cup white wine

Preparation time 30 minutes
Cooking time 30 minutes
Level easy
Wine well-structured, full-bodied white with aromatic flavors,
such as Tuscany Chardonnay Barrique

Heat the oil in a large saucepan and add the shallot. Sauté until softened.

Remove the skin, as well as any bones, from the salt cod. Add the fish to the saucepan with the shallot. Add the potatoes and the milk and cook for 20 to 30 minutes. If the mixture becomes too thick, add a little warm water. Remove from heat and add the parsley. Puree the mixture and season to taste with salt and pepper. Pour into a glass baking dish and refrigerate for 1 hour.

Meanwhile briefly sauté the peaches in a nonstick pan. Add the lemon juice and white wine and let reduce. Puree the mixture and set aside.

Using a cookie cutter, cut out circles of the chilled cod mixture. Place each circle on a serving plate and drizzle with the peach sauce. Serve immediately.

Rice Mille-feuille with Salmon and Zucchini

Serves 4

Mille-feuille
1 small bunch of mixed herbs (thyme, chervil, chives), finely chopped
6 tablespoons extra-virgin olive oil
salt and pepper
6 sheets of frozen rice-paper wrappers (see note)
sunflower oil for frying
8½ ounces smoked salmon, thinly sliced
2 zucchini

Garnish
3½ ounces ricotta salata, grated

Preparation time 25 minutes
Cooking time 10 minutes
Level easy
Wine Medium-bodied white with light grassy undertones,
such as Friuli Isonzo Pinot Grigio

Mix the herbs with the extra-virgin olive oil, season with salt and pepper, and set aside.

Thaw the rice-paper wrappers and cut them into triangles. Heat the sunflower oil and fry the rice-paper triangles for 10 seconds, turning them only once, then drain on paper towels.

Trim the smoked salmon slices to the same size as the rice triangles.

Wash the zucchini and slice very thinly on the diagonal using a mandoline.

Make the mille-feuille by alternating layers of fried rice triangles, smoked salmon, and zucchini, drizzling each layer with the herb oil. Top with grated ricotta salata.

Cook's tip Rice-paper wrappers can be found in Asian food shops and specialty stores. They can be replaced with wonton wrappers.

Roasted Pepper and Octopus Rolls

CAPERS

Capers come from a shrub with fleshy leaves and white flowers. The plant grows wild around the Mediterranean. The capers themselves are the plant's flower buds, picked while still closed. They can be preserved in salt, vinegar, or brine.

Serves 4

Rolls

1 octopus, approximately 2 pounds
½ cup white wine
1 rosemary sprig
½ lemon
salt and pepper
3 roasted red bell peppers
4 tablespoons extra-virgin olive oil
1 tablespoon white wine vinegar
1 dried red chili pepper
1 tablespoon capers in vinegar
1 small bunch of parsley, minced
1 marjoram sprig, minced

Garnish

lamb's lettuce or frisée

Preparation time 30 minutes
Cooking time 40 minutes
Level medium
Wine well-structured white,
such as Campania Fiano di Avellino

Place the octopus in a large pot with 12 cups (3 quarts) water, the wine, rosemary, and lemon half. Lightly salt, cover, and simmer for about 40 minutes, until octopus is tender. Turn off the heat and let cool in the cooking water.

Cut the roasted peppers into ¾-inch-long strips.

Drain the octopus, reserving ½ cup of the cooking water. Cut the octopus tentacles into small pieces and roll each piece in a roasted pepper strip. Secure the rolls with a toothpick if necessary.

Heat the olive oil in a large frying pan and add the octopus rolls. Gently sauté the rolls for a few minutes. Add the vinegar, reserved octopus cooking liquid, and salt, then crumble in the chili pepper. Add the capers, parsley, and marjoram and remove from heat.

Serve the rolls on a bed of lamb's lettuce or frisée.

Cod-Stuffed Artichokes with Crispy Polenta

Serves 4

Artichokes
12 medium artichokes
juice of 1 lemon
3 tablespoons extra-virgin olive oil
1 garlic clove
marjoram
salt
½ cup white wine
1 tablespoon chopped parsley

Cod
4 cups (1 quart) milk
1 bay leaf
1 garlic clove
salt and pepper
10½ ounces fresh cod fillet
3 tablespoons extra-virgin olive oil

Polenta
7 ounces prepared polenta, chilled
1¼ cups sunflower oil
salt

Preparation time 40 minutes
Cooking time 40 minutes
Level medium
Wine young, light-bodied, fragrant rosé, such as Alto Adige Lagrein Rosato

Trim the artichokes, discarding the hard outer leaves, cutting off the spiny tips, and scooping out and discarding the choke. Immerse the trimmed artichokes in a bowl of water with the lemon juice. In a large, shallow saucepan heat the olive oil together with the whole garlic clove and marjoram. Arrange the artichokes in the pan, stalk down, and season with salt. Add the wine, cover, and let cook for 20 to 25 minutes.

Pour the milk into a large saucepan; add the bay leaf, garlic clove, and pinches of salt and pepper; bring to a boil. Add the cod and simmer over low heat for 15 minutes. Remove the fish with a slotted spoon and puree in a food processor or blender. Pour in the olive oil in a thin stream and blend to emulsify. Season with salt and pepper.

Cut the polenta into small, irregular pieces and fry them in hot sunflower oil until crisp. Drain on paper towels and lightly salt. Drain the artichokes, reserving the cooking liquid. Place a spoonful of the cod puree in the center of each artichoke, and arrange the artichokes on a serving plate with the crispy polenta. Strain the artichoke cooking liquid and add the parsley and a few drops of extra-virgin olive oil. Drizzle over the artichokes before serving.

Poached Seafood with Fruit Salad

Serves 4

1¼ cups (5½ ounces) diced celery, carrot, and onion
½ cup white wine
juice and zest of 1 lemon
parsley
8 small red shrimp
4 jumbo shrimp
4 black tiger shrimp
4 langoustines
¼ pineapple, peeled, cored, and chopped
1 kiwi, peeled and sliced
5–6 strawberries, hulled and quartered
1 bunch of salad leaves, torn
3 tablespoons extra-virgin olive oil
ground white pepper
pink peppercorns

Preparation time 20 minutes
Cooking time 30 minutes
Level easy
Wine full-bodied, well-structured, blanc de blancs Champagne,
such as Champagne Brut

Place the celery, carrot, and onion in a saucepan. Add the white wine and water and bring to a boil. Add the lemon rind and parsley. Let simmer for 10 minutes, then add all the shrimp and the langoustines and cook for 4 minutes.

Mix together the pineapple, kiwi, strawberries, and salad leaves. Whisk together the lemon juice, olive oil, white pepper, and pink peppercorns. Drain the seafood and serve over the fruit, dressed with the lemon dressing.

Spicy Shellfish Sauté

Serves 4

9 ounces cockles (if available, or substitute with additional clams and mussels)
7 ounces mussels
9 ounces clams
salt
3 tablespoons extra-virgin olive oil
2 garlic cloves, 1 finely minced, 1 halved
1 dried red chili pepper, crumbled
parsley, chopped (photo 1)
½ cup dry white wine
5 cherry tomatoes, quartered
4 slices crusty bread

Preparation time 20 minutes
Cooking time 10 minutes
Level easy
Wine fresh and fragrant, medium-bodied white with grassy accents,
such as Campania Ischia Bianco

Soak and wash the shellfish, changing the water several times. Purge the shellfish by soaking them separately in 3 bowls of salted water for 30 minutes.

Heat the olive oil in a frying pan and sauté the minced garlic, the chili pepper, and a little parsley. Add the cockles, turn up the heat, and cook for 3 minutes. Pour in the wine, let evaporate, and add the mussels and clams. Return to a simmer and add the tomatoes (photo 2) and the remaining parsley, then cover and cook until the shells open. Remove from heat and discard any unopened shells.

Toast the bread and rub with the garlic halves (photo 3). Arrange the pieces of toast on serving plates, pour the hot shellfish over them, and serve.

Cook's tip The purging process is useful for eliminating sand from inside the shellfish; simply washing the outside will not remove it all. Soaking them in salted water makes mollusks "breathe," allowing them to expel any sand.

Tuna and Swordfish Tartare with Fennel

Serves 4

Tartare
7 ounces sushi-grade tuna fillet
7 ounces sushi-grade swordfish fillet
juice of 1 lemon
wild fennel or dill, minced
salt and pepper
extra-virgin olive oil

Parsley flan
1 bunch parsley
1 egg, separated
1 tablespoon whipping cream
2 tablespoons breadcrumbs
1 tablespoon cornstarch

Garnish
1 tomato, washed and diced
salt and pepper
2 tablespoons black olive puree (tapenade)
extra-virgin olive oil

Preparation time 35 minutes
Cooking time 25 minutes
Level easy
Wine well-structured white with a fully developed bouquet,
such as Sicily Chardonnay

Dice the fish into ¼-inch pieces and place in a bowl. Add the lemon juice, wild fennel or dill, salt, pepper, and a drizzle of olive oil.

Spoon the fish into four round molds, such as cookie cutters, cover with plastic wrap, and place a water glass on top of each to press the contents down. Refrigerate for 2 hours.

Meanwhile preheat oven to 350°F.

Blanch the parsley in salted boiling water for 2 minutes to eliminate any bitterness. Drain and squeeze out any excess water. Place 1 cup of the parsley in a food processor with the egg yolk and cream and blend. Stir in the breadcrumbs and let rest for 5 minutes. To complete the parsley flan, beat the egg white until stiff and gently fold into the parsley puree. Sift in the cornstarch, stir well, and then pour the mixture into small buttered aluminum molds. Bake for 20 minutes.

Season the tomato with pinches of salt and pepper.

On each plate, serve the tartare with the parsley flan, cut in half, from one aluminum mold, as well as a spoonful of fresh tomato. Complete each plate with a little tapenade and a drizzle of olive oil.

Salmon Trout and Smoked Sturgeon Roll

Serves 4

Roll
2 salmon trout fillets (or 2 salmon fillets)
fresh thyme, chopped
pepper
7 ounces smoked sturgeon, sliced
1 red bell pepper
6 tablespoons delicate extra-virgin olive oil
poppy seeds

Potatoes
2 potatoes, peeled
½ cup vegetable broth
1 packet powdered saffron
salt
a small piece of Savoy cabbage, diced

Garnish
1 tablespoon pine nuts
basil, salt, and pepper
sunflower oil for frying
2 tomatoes

Preparation time 35 minutes
Cooking time 40 minutes
Level medium
Wine medium-bodied white with aromatic vegetal notes and hints of yellow fruits, such as Marche Verdicchio di Matelica

Debone the trout fillets and butterfly them using a very sharp knife. Season with thyme and pepper, then place the sturgeon slices over the trout fillets. Wash the bell pepper and julienne three-quarters of it, setting the remaining piece aside. Heat 2 tablespoons of olive oil in a frying pan and sauté the julienned pepper until the strips begin to soften. Arrange the pepper strips on top of the sturgeon and roll up. Wrap the rolls in plastic wrap, twisting the ends like the wrapper on a piece of candy. Steam the trout rolls for 7 minutes and let cool slightly.

Using a melon baller, make 16 small balls from the potatoes. Boil the potato balls in the broth with the saffron and a pinch of salt. Meanwhile roast and peel the remaining piece of bell pepper. Dice it and mix with the cabbage. As soon as the potato balls are done, drain and roll them in the pepper-cabbage mixture. Puree the pine nuts, basil, salt, and pepper with a little sunflower oil to make a light pesto.

Blanch the tomatoes and cool them in ice water; gently peel them and fry their skins in sunflower oil. Unwrap the trout roll, sprinkle with the poppy seeds, and cut into thick slices. Serve with the potato balls, fried tomato skins, and pesto.

Shrimp in Brandy Sauce

Serves 4

2 ripe tomatoes
1 shallot, minced
2 tablespoons extra-virgin olive oil
1 ¼ pounds jumbo shrimp
¼ cup brandy
½ cup white wine
salt and pepper
½ cup light cream
parsley, chopped

Preparation time 15 minutes
Cooking time 15 minutes
Level easy
Wine well-structured white with persistent flavors,
such as Tuscany Bolgheri Bianco

Blanch tomatoes in boiling water for 30 seconds, then peel and coarsely chop.

Gently sauté the shallot in a frying pan with the olive oil and 2 to 3 tablespoons of water until golden and soft.

Add the shrimp to the pan and let cook for 2 to 3 minutes. Pour in the brandy, let evaporate, then add the white wine and reduce to half the original volume.

Add the chopped tomato, salt, and pepper and cook for about 10 minutes. Remove the shrimp and set them aside.

Add the cream to the cooking liquid and let the mixture reduce over high heat. Season the sauce with salt and pepper, add the parsley, and serve the shrimp with the brandy sauce.

Cook's tip This appetizer can become a tasty main course by serving the shrimp with a small timbale of boiled basmati rice.

Oysters with "Black Oil" and Citron

Serves 4

1 cup (5 ounces) black olives, pitted
6 tablespoons extra-virgin olive oil
white pepper
8 oysters, shells scrubbed
juice and grated zest of 1 citron
  (or lemon)

Preparation time 10 minutes
Cooking time 2 hours
Level easy
Wine Well-structured Champagne
with a full, rich bouquet, such as
Champagne Cuvée de Prestige

OYSTERS

The best way to prepare oysters is to open them just before eating, using an oyster knife with a short, thick blade and hand guard. Place the knife tip in the ridged edge of the shell, taking care to protect the hand holding the oyster by covering it with a folded towel.

Preheat oven to 175°F.

Halve the olives, place them on a baking sheet (preferably perforated), and let dry in the oven for 2 hours. Remove and let cool completely.

Place the olives in a blender or food processor with the olive oil and a little white pepper, then puree to form a smooth paste. Pass the mixture through a fine-mesh sieve.

Open the oysters and place them on a bed of ice. Sprinkle with a few drops of citron juice and a pinch of grated zest. Add a drizzle of the black oil and serve immediately.

Variation The oysters may also be breaded and broiled. Briefly sauté a garlic clove in a frying pan with olive oil and parsley, add breadcrumbs, and season to taste with salt and pepper. Open the oysters, cover them with the seasoned breadcrumbs, and broil on high for a couple of minutes.

Shrimp-Stuffed Sole

Serves 4

2 potatoes, peeled and julienned
squid ink
8 shelled shrimp, tails left on
2 fresh sole, filleted and cut into 8 strips
juice of 1 orange
1 small bunch of parsley
sunflower oil for frying
salt
6 tablespoons extra-virgin olive oil
pink peppercorns
1 spring onion, white part only, chopped

Preparation time 35 minutes
Cooking time 25 minutes
Level easy
Wine medium-bodied white with a developed bouquet of yellow fruits,
such as Trentino Müller Thurgau

Soak the julienned potatoes in cold water, changing the water several times. Drain and place half of the potatoes in a bowl with the squid ink and a little water. Let sit.

Place one shrimp on each fillet strip, with the tail hanging over the edge. Roll up the fillet so the tail sticks out of the center of the roll.

Place the orange juice, parsley, and a little water in a large pot. Bring to a boil and place a vegetable steamer in the pot. Steam the sole rolls, covered, for about 8 minutes.

Drain all of the potatoes and fry in hot sunflower oil. Drain and season to taste with salt.

Meanwhile mix the olive oil with the pink peppercorns, a pinch of salt, and the chopped spring onion. Serve the sole rolls with the fried potatoes and seasoned oil.

Savory Salmon Tart

Serves 4

Dough

2 teaspoons active dry yeast
$2/3$ cup lukewarm water
2 tablespoons extra-virgin olive oil
salt
$2^1/_3$ cups (10½ ounces) all-purpose flour

Stuffing

1 potato
3 zucchini, sliced into rounds
1 bunch of Swiss chard
6 tablespoons extra-virgin olive oil
salt and white pepper
7 ounces salmon fillet, thinly sliced
thyme

Preparation time 20 minutes
Cooking time 40 minutes
Level easy
Wine well-structured white with excellent aromatic persistence,
such as Alto Adige Gewürztraminer

Preheat oven to 375°F.

Dissolve the yeast in the lukewarm water and add the olive oil and salt. Mound the flour on a work surface and make a well in the center. Add the yeast mixture and knead to form a smooth and elastic dough. Cover with a clean kitchen towel and let sit.

Boil the potato, and blanch the zucchini and Swiss chard separately in salted water. Drain and squeeze out excess water from the Swiss chard. Slice the potato.

Butter and flour a pie pan and line it with rolled dough; pierce the dough with a fork.

Arrange the Swiss chard on the dough and season with a drizzle of oil and a pinch of white pepper. Make a second layer with the potato slices and season again. Layer thin slices of salmon on top of the potatoes and then top with the blanched zucchini rounds. Season with pinches of salt and thyme, and drizzle with olive oil. Bake for 40 minutes. Remove from heat and cool completely. Serve cold.

Broiled Scallops with Lemon Thyme

Serves 4

4 tablespoons extra-virgin olive oil
2 garlic cloves
8 tablespoons breadcrumbs
1 sprig lemon thyme, leaves only
2 baby zucchini, cut into rounds
salt and pepper
4 large scallops
6 small scallops

Preparation time 15 minutes
Cooking time 5 minutes
Level easy
Wine medium-bodied white with fresh and fragrant aromas, such as Calabria Cirò Bianco

LEMON THYME

This herb is similar to wild thyme but bears a marked lemon fragrance. Lemon thyme pairs well with fish, eggs, and lamb.

Preheat broiler.

Heat 3 tablespoons of the olive oil in a nonstick pan with the unpeeled garlic cloves. Sauté briefly, then remove the garlic and add the breadcrumbs. Toast for a few minutes, then transfer to a bowl and stir in the lemon thyme.

In another pan, heat the remaining olive oil and sauté the zucchini. Season with salt and pepper, remove from heat, and let cool slightly.

Wash the scallops and remove the thin black thread. Wash the shells and place the scallops back in their shells. Top with the sautéed zucchini and cover evenly with breadcrumbs. Broil on high for 5 minutes, or until golden brown. Serve with a drizzle of olive oil.

Salmon and Escarole Mousse

Serves 4

Mousse
3 tablespoons butter
1 shallot, minced
1 dried red chili pepper
1 head of escarole, chopped
14 ounces salmon fillet, chopped
4 tablespoons dry white wine
¼ cup (2 ¼ ounces) black olives, pitted
2 tablespoons salted capers, rinsed
4 tablespoons mayonnaise
salt and pepper

Garnish
4 black olives, pitted and sliced
1 roasted red bell pepper in oil, drained and diced
1 baguette, sliced and toasted

Preparation time 25 minutes
Cooking time 10 minutes
Level easy
Wine medium-bodied white with persistence on the palate,
such as Umbria Orvieto Classico

Melt the butter in a frying pan, add the shallot, and crumble in the chili pepper. Add the escarole and cover and cook for 5 minutes, until the escarole is reduced in volume. Add the salmon, pour in the wine, and let evaporate. Add the olives for the mousse, along with the capers, and continue cooking until the salmon is cooked through.

Let the salmon mixture cool. Transfer to a food processor or blender and add the mayonnaise, salt, and pepper. Blend the mixture to obtain a smooth puree. Transfer to a silicone mold and refrigerate for at least 2 hours.

Remove the mousse from the mold, keeping it intact, and place it on a serving plate. Garnish with the sliced olives and diced bell pepper. Serve with toast.

Cook's tip Escarole is used in this recipe because it makes the mousse softer, and it doesn't lose its consistency during cooking. The slightly bitter flavor also makes a pleasant contrast with the sweeter flavors of the salmon and shallot.

Roasted Pepper and Anchovy Rolls

Serves 4

1 red bell pepper
1 yellow bell pepper
3 tablespoons extra-virgin olive oil
1 garlic clove, halved
5 salted capers, drained, rinsed, and minced
3 tablespoons breadcrumbs
parsley, chopped
salt and pepper
12 anchovy fillets in oil, drained

Preparation time 25 minutes
Cooking time 15 minutes
Level easy
Wine medium-bodied white with marked aromas of yellow fruits,
such as Veneto Chardonnay

Preheat oven to 400°F.

Halve the peppers and remove the seeds and white pith. Roast in a hot oven, under a broiler or directly over the gas flame of a cooker, turning often so that the skin blackens evenly. Transfer to a plastic bag to let steam. When cooled, remove, peel, and cut each half into 3 strips, for a total of 12 slices.

Heat the oil in a frying pan and sauté the garlic until golden. Add the capers, and then the breadcrumbs. Toast over low heat, stirring often. Add the parsley, salt, and pepper. Remove and discard the garlic.

Place an anchovy fillet on top of each pepper slice. Cover with the breadcrumb mixture and roll up, closing with a toothpick. Bake for 4 minutes.

Cook's tip Another way to cook and peel bell peppers is to fry them whole in a pan of hot sunflower oil. It is important not to have the oil too hot so the peppers cook slowly.

Potato Salad with Salmon Roe and Spiced Cream

Serves 4

1 pound new potatoes
salt
4 tablespoons extra-virgin olive oil
1 cup heavy cream
juice of ½ lemon
1 tablespoon mixed ground spices (cloves, cumin, black pepper, star anise)
5½ ounces salmon roe
1 handful of watercress sprouts

Preparation time 20 minutes
Cooking time 30 minutes
Level easy
Wine Lago di Caldaro Schiava

Boil the whole potatoes in salted water until tender. Drain, let cool, and then peel. Cut into wedges and toss with the olive oil and a pinch of salt. Mix together the cream and lemon juice, stirring well until the mixture thickens. Stir in the spices.

Arrange the potatoes in small serving bowls. Top with spiced cream and salmon roe. Garnish with watercress sprouts before serving.

Cook's tip The salmon roe can be replaced by strips of smoked salmon. The cream and lemon juice can also be replaced by a tub of crème fraîche.

Carla Aradelli
Riva

Marcello and
Gianluca Leoni
Il Sole

Alessandra Buriani
Buriani

Silvio Battistoni

Romano Rossi
Il Testamento del Porco

Silvio Battistoni
Ristorante Schuman

Special Recipes

Chefs from the best
Italian restaurants open
their kitchens to reveal
the secrets of the recipes
that made them famous.

Culatello-and-Turbot-Stuffed Squid

from Marcello and Gianluca Leoni

Serves 4

Squid
extra-virgin olive oil
1 tablespoon minced leek
3 ½ ounces turbot fillet, diced
salt and pepper
2 ounces culatello di Zibello or prosciutto, chopped
1 tablespoon grated Parmesan
40 very small baby squid, cleaned
dried chili pepper flakes

Sweet-corn puree
1 cup (5 ounces) fresh sweet-corn kernels
beef stock
salt and pepper

Garnish
1 zucchini, green part only, julienned
extra-virgin olive oil
salt and pepper
4 cherry tomatoes, quartered
balsamic vinegar

Preparation time 20 minutes
Cooking time 20 minutes
Level easy
Wine well-structured white with distinct acidity and sustained body,
such as Friuli Malvasia Istriana

Heat 2 tablespoons of olive oil in a frying pan and add the leek. Sauté until soft, then add the turbot. Season with pinches of salt and pepper and cook for a few minutes. Transfer the mixture to a food processor and add the culatello (or prosciutto) and Parmesan. Puree until smooth, and stuff the mixture into the squid. Sauté the squid in a pan with a little olive oil and the chili pepper.

Boil the fresh sweet corn in salted water until tender. Drain, then puree with a little beef stock. Pass through a sieve and transfer to a nonstick pan. Cook over medium heat until the mixture has thickened. Season to taste with salt and pepper.

Toss the zucchini with extra-virgin olive oil, salt, and pepper.

Place 1 spoonful of sweet-corn puree in the middle of a plate.

Arrange 10 stuffed squid on top and garnish with the zucchini, tomatoes, and a drizzle of balsamic vinegar.

Savory French Toast with Creamy Pesto
from Carla Aradelli

Serves 8

Creamy pesto
1 ½ teaspoons pine nuts
3 basil leaves
2 tablespoons extra-virgin olive oil
5 ounces ricotta
3 ½ ounces fresh goat cheese
salt and pepper

Toast
2 eggs
2 tablespoons grated Parmesan
salt and pepper
1 loaf of bread (about 11 ounces), sliced
½ cup milk
4 tablespoons (2 ounces) butter

Vegetables
4 asparagus spears
1 cup (4 ounces) green beans
3 tablespoons peas
1 small zucchini
4 spring onions
3 tablespoons extra-virgin olive oil
salt

Preparation time 15 minutes
Cooking time 5 minutes
Level easy
Wine young light-bodied red with notes of red fruits and herbs,
such as Oltrepò Pavese Barbera

Crush the pine nuts and basil using a mortar and pestle. Add the olive oil, ricotta, goat cheese, salt, and pepper. Set aside in a cool place.

Beat together the eggs, Parmesan, salt, and pepper. Soak the bread slices in milk, then dip them into the egg mixture. Melt the butter in a saucepan and fry the slices of bread. Remove from pan and cut into small strips.

Blanch the asparagus and the green beans together with the peas. Cut all of the vegetables into julienne strips, discarding the white part of the zucchini. Sauté the vegetables together briefly in olive oil and season with salt.

Arrange the vegetables in a circle on individual serving plates. Arrange the slices of French toast on the plates and top with dollops of creamy pesto.

Shrimp with Salama da Sugo, Melon, and Yogurt

from Alessandra Buriani

Serves 4

Shrimp
20 shrimp, peeled but with heads attached
aromatic herbs, chopped
extra-virgin olive oil
salt and pepper
mixed greens
1 salama da sugo, or cotto salami (cooked salami), julienned
1 small melon, julienned

Sauce
2 tablespoons plain yogurt
extra-virgin olive oil
salt and pepper
1 piece of fresh ginger, grated

Preparation time 30 minutes
Cooking time 10 minutes
Level easy
Wine medium-bodied white with a refined and elegant bouquet,
such as Alto Adige Chardonnay

Sprinkle the shrimp with the aromatic herbs, then steam them until tender. Toss with extra-virgin olive oil, and season with pinches of salt and pepper.

Wash the mixed salad leaves, dry them and wrap in a clean kitchen towel, then refrigerate for a few minutes to crisp.

Mix yogurt with a drizzle of olive oil, salt, pepper, and ginger. Remove the lettuce from the refrigerator and dress with the yogurt dressing.

Using a cookie cutter to shape, arrange the salad, shrimp, salama da sugo, and melon on the plate. Drizzle with any remaining yogurt dressing to complete the dish, and serve immediately.

Cook's tip Salama da sugo is a typical salami from the Ferrara area. Sometimes called salamina, it dates back to the fifteenth century. When not available, it can be replaced with salame cotto, cooked salami.

Puff Pastry with Porcini Mushrooms and Bacon

from Romano Rossi

Serves 4

14 ounces puff pastry
salt and pepper
1 tablespoon extra-virgin olive oil
1 shallot, minced
1 garlic clove, minced
4 medium porcini mushrooms
½ cup dry white wine
2 tablespoons béchamel
16 slices of pancetta or bacon
parsley, minced

Preparation time 20 minutes
Cooking time 15 minutes
Level easy
Wine young, light-bodied red wine with distinct aromas of red fruits,
such as Veneto Bardolino Classico

Preheat oven to 425°F.

Lightly salt the puff pastry, cut it into 4-inch squares, and bake until golden brown.

Heat the olive oil in a frying pan, add the shallot and garlic, and sauté for a few minutes.

Remove and discard the earthy stalk of the mushrooms. Wipe the mushrooms well with a damp cloth and thinly slice, then add to the frying pan. Pour in the white wine, let evaporate, then continue cooking (adding vegetable stock if the mixture becomes too dry) until the mushrooms are done. Season to taste with salt and pepper, then stir in the béchamel.

Microwave the bacon slices for 40 seconds on maximum power to make them crisp.

Plate by layering puff pastry squares, spoonfuls of mushrooms, and slices of bacon. Finish with a puff pastry square and some bacon. Sprinkle with parsley and serve.

Parmesan and Black Truffle Soufflé

from Silvio Battistoni

Serves 4

Soufflé

3 ½ tablespoons butter
6 ½ tablespoons all-purpose flour
2 cups milk
4 eggs, 1 separated
1 black Norcia truffle, grated
1 cup (3 ½ ounces) grated Parmesan cheese
salt and pepper

Sauce

¾ cup plus 1 tablespoon heavy cream
2 ounces Taleggio cheese
salt and pepper
2 tablespoons butter
3 tablespoons grated Parmesan cheese

Preparation time 50 minutes
Cooking time 30 minutes
Level easy
Wine well-structured white with marked flavors of yellow fruits,
such as Sicily Bianco d'Alcamo

Preheat the oven to 400°F.

Melt the butter in a saucepan and stir in the flour to make a roux. Let cook for 5 minutes, then remove from the heat and let cool. Bring the milk to a boil, then whisk into the roux to make a béchamel. Stir in 3 eggs and 1 egg yolk.

Beat the remaining egg white to soft peaks, then fold into the mixture together with a little of the truffle and the Parmesan. Season with salt and pepper.

Butter individual ramekins and lightly dust with flour. Pour in the batter and bake for 20 minutes.

Meanwhile make the sauce by bringing the cream to a boil with the cheese and stirring until it melts. Adjust salt and pepper, then whisk in the butter to make the sauce shiny.

To serve, pour a little of the sauce on a plate, then unmold a soufflé on top. Sprinkle with the remaining truffle and a little grated Parmesan.

Chefs' Tools

A FEW, SIMPLE, STURDY, AND VALUABLE UTENSILS WILL HELP YOU PREPARE DELICIOUS AND ATTRACTIVE APPETIZERS.

1 **Flat whisk** The design of this whisk, which is much flatter than a traditional whisk, makes it ideal for mixing small quantities. This utensil is perfect for whisking vinaigrettes, liquid sauces, and creams, as well as for making extra-fluffy omelets.

2 **Beater** This special small, round steel-wire whisk is essential for getting rid of lumps in liquids, even in narrow vessels.

3 **"Grana" knife** A knife with a sturdy steel blade designed specifically to cut hard cheeses.

4 **Melon baller** An implement for scooping the flesh out of fruits and vegetables in the form of perfectly shaped spheres.

5 **Scissor-shaped tongs** With these easy-to-grip serving tongs, you won't drop an olive or canapé again.

6 **Grater and slicer** As the name suggests, this single device can give you the ability to grate cheese and julienne vegetables—perfect for preparing a visually appealing and delicious salads.

Glossary

Bisque
A French term for a soup usually made with crabs, crayfish, shrimp, lobsters, or langoustines. There is no single recipe, and many different ingredients can be included.

Court bouillon
A slightly acidic broth, flavored with vegetables, aromatic herbs, and spices, often used to poach seafood.

Filleting
The process of cutting fillets away from the middle and side bones of a fish and separating one fillet from the other. A sharp knife with a thin and flexible blade is needed. You can often have this done for you when you purchase fish.

Kombu seaweed
A brown seaweed rich in minerals. When cooked with beans, it makes them tenderer and easier to digest.

Lemon thyme
A particular kind of thyme possessing a flavor more delicate than common thyme, as well as a distinctive citrus fragrance. Lemon thyme is used to season salads and other vegetable dishes.

Marinade
Used for preserving foods or adding more flavor to them. A classic marinade is prepared with wine (white or red), vinegar, and oil, as well as vegetables and aromatic herbs such as onions, carrots, shallots, bay leaves, juniper berries, and cloves.

Nori seaweed
A red seaweed, also known as sea lettuce. It is often sold in dried sheets which are made from the pulped seaweed that has been poured into square molds, arranged over bamboo mats, and sun-dried or baked in large ovens.

Pastry bag
A plastic or cloth cone that can be filled with sauces and mixtures to pipe onto culinary creations.

Quenelle

An oval dumpling, shaped by hand or with the help of two spoons. It is made with forcemeat (usually fish).

Rice vinegar

A vinegar made from the fermentation of rice flours and subsequent acetic fermentation.

Tahini

A paste made with ground sesame seeds. In Middle Eastern and Greek cuisine, it's served as an appetizer. It is usually sold in jars and can be found in specialty shops and large supermarkets.

Index

Printed in China in September 2008